DRIFTING

THE TAIWANESE
MODERN LITERATURE SERIES
Edited by Dominic Cheung

Supported by a matching grant from
the Council for Cultural Affairs in Taiwan

Drifting Dominic Cheung (Chang Ts'o)

forthcoming

*Erotic Recipes: A Complete Menu
for Male Potency Enhancement* Jiao Tong

Drifting

Dominic Cheung
(CHANG TS'O)

GREEN INTEGER
KØBENHAVN & LOS ANGELES
2000

GREEN INTEGER BOOKS
Edited by Per Bregne
København/Los Angeles

Distributed in the United States by Consortium Book
Sales and Distribution, 1045 Westgate Drive, Suite 90
Saint Paul, Minnesota 55114-1065

(323) 857-1115/http://www.greeninteger.com

First Green Integer Edition 2000
©1986 by Dominic Cheung
English language translation ©2000 by Dominic Cheung
Back cover copy ©2000 by Green Integer

Design: Per Bregne
Typography: Guy Bennett
Cover: Photograph of Dominic Cheung by Stella Yaya

Publication of this book was made possible, in part, through a grant
from the The Council for Cultural Affairs in Taiwan
and the California Arts Council

LIBRARY OF CONGRESS CATALOGING IN PUBLICATION DATA
Cheung, Dominic (Chang Ts'o)
Drifting
ISBN: 1-892295-71-7
p. cm — Green Integer 79
I. Title II. Series

The Modern Taiwanese Literature Series

As a professional poet and an avid reader of poetry, I have often been frustrated by the experience of reading an anthology in translation, in which the appreciation of poems is totally dissociated from the recognition of poets. On the other hand, reading an anthology of Asian poetry, Western readers tend to focus on the content of the poems more than on the unfamiliar names of the poets. Occasionally, an editor or a translator may attach brief historical accounts or short biographies, but the logical effect of connecting poems to hard-to-remember foreign names is still lacking. Furthermore, an anthology often falls short of presenting a poet's spectrum of poetic variants within his or her work.

As a solution to the above dilemma, I proposed to the Council for Cultural Affairs in Taiwan to translate a series of five individual volumes of poetry in Chinese, namely, poetry selections from modern Taiwanese poets (Chinese surnames first) Chang Ts'o, Hsi Muren, Chen Yi-chih, Jiao Tong, and Hsu Hui-chih. The above list represents two generations of poets who play an active role in the making of modern Chinese poetry in Taiwan in the past two decades.

Serving as the chief editor of the above series, and with the help of the associate editor Jiao Tong, I have collected poems from the respective poets, and in turn assigned them to qualified translators. I went through each translated poem carefully and consulted with the translators whenever doubts arose. Thus I should be held solely responsible for any textual negligence and translation errors.

Last but not least, I wish to thank my colleagues Ron Gottesman and James Ragan at USC who introduced me to Douglas Messerli, poet-publisher of Sun & Moon Press and Green Integer. The name Sun & Moon that reminds people of a scenic spot in Taiwan is not a pure coincidence; it also means "brightness" when these two Chinese characters are combined. Douglas and his Green Integer series have indeed brought a bright future to the modern poetry of Taiwan.

—DOMINIC CHEUNG
University of Southern California

Contents

Foreword   9

Fragrant Herbs by the Orchid Stream   15
Love Poems of Tea   18
The Legend of Tea   20
Drinking Tea   22
To the Hosts: A Reply   25
Empty Promises   27
Confused   29
Reliance   31
Double Jade Pendant Grievance   33
Autumn Meditation   36
Chrysanthemums   40
Mountain Dwelling   42
On Reading Keats' "Ode on a Grecian Urn"   44
Reading *Tao Te Ching*, Chapter 20   47
Window   49
A Willow Leaf Double Saber   51
Blue Seas and Mulberry Fields   54
Wu-hui Monogatari   57

Midnight Is My Song 59

Reincarnation 62

The Panther 65

Tiburon, California 67

Dream Cutting Sword 70

Pink Cheeks 72

Redondo Beach in Evening Rain 74

Promises 76

Cliff House 78

One After My Own Heart 81

Outflow 84

A Name Seal 86

The Watch 88

Heidegger! Heidegger! 91

A Fish Fossil 95

Beauty of Imperfection 100

Yearning 102

Maple Leaf Watermarks 105

The Last Love Poem 109

Foreword

Most of the poems in this volume, except for a few which appeared in my earlier works, are translations from my collection of poems—*Drifters* (first edition, Taipei, 1986). If life indeed consists of segments of histories, *Drifters* represents a life segment in which I found myself deeply distressed by a sense of the diaspora, a misplacement of time and space, and a feeling of helplessness regarding fleeting life and love. *Drifters* was well received in Taiwan and soon progressed onto its second edition. Meanwhile, it has also received Taiwan's most coveted literary award, the *National Literature and Arts Prize* in 1989.

I first came to America in 1967 as a graduate student in English. At the age of 23, I had already published two volumes of poetry and a volume of prose in Chinese before coming to the States. Writing poems in English had imbued with me a spirit of the cosmopolitan, an American dream that I could be part of the melting pot process. But I soon discovered that the precision of language, and the insistence of such, as an expression in poetry, was more important than the persistence of my ethnic identity. Wasting no time, I wrote mainly in Chinese again. Many years later, I realized that I had become an American writing in Chinese. I live in America but I have published more than thirty books in Taiwan, Hong Kong, and China. Sometimes I ponder on whether am I a Chinese poet, an Asian American writer, both, or none of the above?

However, in translating these poems into English, a language that I have dealt with bilingually for the past thirty-some years, I have gone through a "re-creating" experience that is quite unique to a writer. With these poems, I have a total liberty to search for the ultimate meaning behind the meaning of words, and consequently, I found myself immersed into a different self to speak in another voice, so that all intended meaning could be exhausted through the process of translating. I found myself speaking differently, in another medium so to speak, and in that process have recreated new meanings. And yet more often than not, I have constantly restrained myself within the target language and clung stubbornly to the original text.

Thus I begin to realize the possibility and impossibility of translating poetry. Poetry is an art of hiding. The better the poem, the more skillful the hider. He conceals his intention so artfully that only images and metaphors are to be traced. In fact, the less he reveals, the more he intends to mean. Sometimes, he may speak more, but more only in the sense of "enveloping" or "developing" into another message. During the 1980s, I was once intensely caught up by the practice of the "Projective Verse." Charles Olson's "field composition" in which "One perception must immediately and directly lead in a further perception" impressed me greatly. I read many of W.C. Williams' works as well, and particularly in *Paterson,* his epical scheme of locality and the dislocation of syntax fascinated me.

Nevertheless, these poems represent a journey

of my drifting, and someone else perhaps, physically and mentally. Somewhat like Matthew Arnold's lines, we wander in between two worlds. However, instead of one world dead and the other powerless to be born, I wander in between the worlds of the East and the West, back and forth, one not totally dead, the other too powerful to be overwhelmed. It is also a drifting of a Taoist paradox. For many years have I longed for a home and a nation, and after many years, I find myself still searching. A kind of utopian search, I guess, beginning with a bit of the real but ending up largely with the unreal. I yearn for a dwelling of the body and mind where the spirit burgeons.

Like duckweeds floating in a river, they may gather for a while but soon find themselves drifting apart. The fingers of fate rake on a river like a gentle breeze, passing through the duckweeds. Weeds gather and depart in the wind, like people in this world, drifting in the river of time.

It is a sentimental journey once again to go through these poems that I have written many years ago. Like life reincarnations, they remind me of someone or something so familiar, yet so faraway. However, I am responsible for their present appearances in English, no matter how differently they appeared in Chinese in their past lives.

—DOMINIC CHEUNG
(CHANG TS'O)

Fragrant Herbs by the Orchid Stream

Returning from China's northern border
A friend brought me a Tibetan knife
Sheathed in golden copper
A blade is slender like water
The graceful knife is an orchid leaf.
They say, Tibetans sat in a circle,
Cut meat, and drank wine…
There was a night in a courtyard,
The cold, enchanted knife flashed amidst the moon-
    light
A slash of the sharp, silvery blade
Like a broken icicle, plunging, splashing
White lights bouncing in the hand
A knife cutting meat can slaughter dragons
And take off a tyrant's head!
Vaguely I hear a thousand miles away,
The rumbling of thunder and wind, a song:
"Gray, gray, the sky
Wide, wide the plain

When the wind blows, the grass is swept low
Faraway, you see cattle grazing."
You can almost hear whips snapping in the air
Horses perspiring blood, rushing into the sunset.
A thick layer of cloud mist befalls
And links long reeds to the horizon;
They had finally led horses to the stream
Where the murmuring water tells an eternal tale:
In golden palaces within the four major regions
Where Dalai, Panchen, and other Lamas stayed,
The Potala in Lhasa was the palace monastery
A fortress of peasants' sweat and blood;
One year by the lake,
An old Lama prayed for three days and nights
And found the most esteemed Dalai reincarnated
In a stony cabin with green tiles.
But the *Han* Chinese brought in liberation and
        suppression,
Modernization and pollution,
Recovery and hatred;
The long, long road,
Tearing out the heart of the green, green plain.
Drifting outcries,

Homeless fears,
Patriotic worries,
Vaguely I hold this Tibetan knife in my palm,
No one knows of my martial skill.
Loneliness is an orchid by the stream
Which I wish to pluck and give to someone
Someone is far, far away.
I turn and look homeward
The road is long and wide
Deep in the vale, a leaf of orchid by the swamp
Deep in one's hand, a knife made in Tibet
Forever waiting,
For the summons of the faraway native land!

Love Poems of Tea

1
If I, the boiling water,
And you, the tea;
Then your fragrance
Has to depend solely upon my plainness.

2
Let your dryness inside me
Softly uncoil and stretch;
Let me dissolve
Imperceptibly, your tension.

3
I have to be hot, even boiled
Before we consume each other;
We have to hide, see and hold
each other in water
to decide
a tea color.

4
No matter how capriciously
you drift;
Gradually and slowly
(O' gently)
You will into me submerge—
Deep.

5
By that moment
The most bitter tear of yours
will become a best sip
of my fragrance.

The Legend of Tea

It was told that
When the monk awoke
Like crisscrossing footprints
On deserted mountains and snowy hills,
Traces of his dream emerged before his very eyes.
Feeling repentant and restless
He snipped the thick, sleep-tempting eyelashes
From his thick, bearded face.
Accordingly, in a single night
Shrubs of bitter tea began to grow;
They can restrain the hot tempers of the secular man
And cravings of the religious monk.

But from a sip of tea, how can I fully taste
The first half of a spring night?
From the tiny broken floral pattern of a blue porce-
    lain cup
How can I trace the change of tea color and its
    astringency?

How can I, also, search and discover the dried, knitted
      thoughts
From the submerging and the surfacing tea leaves?

"While tea is still warm
You have left."
Each time, you grieved,
"The tea is as thick
As my homesick nostalgia."
Every time, you also said,
"Tea was made only once, and you left
The teapot and hot water
Remain our mountain vows, our ocean love."
The monk finally sighed
Shrubs of tea are pages of unsolved *koan*
Turning secular laymen and holy monks to ponder
Between tea and meal
From morning bell to evening drum—
"You came all the way to the West
What does that mean?
What does that mean?"

Drinking Tea

It was said that
Should you want tea
You follow the stony path, covered
With verdant moss;
Coming upon a drooping, thatched roof
Stooping, and
Stepping high over the threshold
You enter amidst the thicket of bamboo
A cottage for tea.

It was also said,
You must wash your hands
Cleanse your thoughts
Release all worldly dust
To the murmuring waters of the bamboo tubes
Until your mind is pure.
Accordingly,
Garments are of simple colors
And some things must not be mentioned—

Money, religion,
In-laws, wars, gossip—
None have to do with the drinking of tea.

Since the tea cottage resides beyond worldliness
You should know the marvels of *sabi* and *wabi*
When you hold the bowl with both hands
Tip your head back, and drain the tea;
You should learn the history of the tea bowl
And its high aesthetics,
As you converse
Your intermittent surprises and compliments
Have to concern the bowl and its possessor,
Since among the tea bowls
Is the encounter of predecessor and successor.

"Such an old, simple Shino bowl
The dense, dark spreading dots
Resemble the blue mountain after rain."
Such commentary is only the layman's.
Because, though in making and drinking tea
You may define the role of the host and his guests

And the levels of tea tastes
Only the simplicity of the tea bowl
Can soothe the relation of the tea drinkers,
A master once remarked,
"Be sure you know
That the tea ceremony, in essence,
Is simply
To boil water,
Make tea, and drink it."
Such a simple matter
Can turn someone to insist on everlasting
        romance—
The red tinge on the bowl's rim
Recalls from early years, red lips.

To the Hosts: A Reply

—For Takuro

After strenuous cultivation
We may sit under a tree
Drink tea, and comment on the sparse, seasonal
    cherries.
There is nothing to be blamed
On the summer cherry
Which once blossomed with weeping flowers;
Having gone through adverse weather
Having borne unto death a stubborn beauty
The flowers are finally infatuated by spring
With a cry:
Love and separation!

This is like the spew of crimson blood
Spat on the lone darkness of night.
This is why, my friend,
We will not trace any bedtime romance
Nor blame any foreign exiles
For the bitter suffering of lonesome cherries.

This is why, my hostess
Once you've made the chrysanthemum tea
And hold the bowl to drink by the fireside
Do not forget to recall the heroic suffering of a
        weeping tree
The crackling flowers outside the sill
Will echo with exegeses,
This is why, my dear couple,
In this emotionless age
We use cherry for red lips,
In this age of belief
We use fallen petals for drifting years,
In this age of patriotism
We use the sword instead of scriptures.

Empty Promises

> *Coming is an empty promise*
> *Leaving is without any trace.*
> —LI SHANG-YIN
> (813–858 AD)

Since I have given my life to you
What else is there to regret and hope for?
Perhaps everything is an empty promise
Like your arrival, abrupt but gentle
As a breeze over my body, cooling and soothing
Sweeping the green fields of early spring;
The beginning is a widespread disturbance
In the end, there are waves and waves
Of restive mood.

Since this life of ours, I know, is over
What is there to say of our next life?
Really, empty promises are empty
Like the silence of your departure
And my sudden waking from a dream.
I persist in searching your scent on the pillows

Among the blossoming flowers of the bed sheets
But in my own blooming, bitter smile
Is the taste of a heartbroken red cherry.

Since both word and action are empty, without trace
Why would I wake, and, still, turn to look at you
And be filled with helpless joy?
I seem to have died
Or suffered a terrible disaster;
I wake and, upon your return, we look at each other,
You, vainly; I, wordless.
All right. Everything is like a play you have promised
     me:
When you really want to go
The show was already over.

Confused

Only at that very moment,
My mind was all confused.
　　　—LI SHANG-YIN

Such an easy phrase
Such a touching word
It will, in midnight remorse, even make you cry,
Or rush outdoors in an early dawn
To confront the new spring in melting snow
And cast coldly a glance at the world—

Simply for love confused.
You are prepared to erase your life
For the sake of those very moments when
Flowers silently bloom
Rivers abruptly bend
Mountains in awesome reflections;
Hands touch each other
Foreheads tap gently together
And eyes meet, to charm.
At last, you hastily give over your life

One tedious and helpless
With confused moments.
Yes, one life have you
Yet, have you one love to give,
To sing, and to remember?
Yes, one death to die you have,
But do life and death only repeat a song,
Again and again, repeating one single theme?
Handfuls of heroic feelings have you,
But you have only a single choice of devotion.
Whatever happened, what you recall
In trauma or in intermittent sobs,
Those are the very moments, the innumerable
        confusions
When you have only duty to oblige.

Reliance

The spring heart of Emperor Wang
Relies on the crying of the cuckoos.
—LI SHANG-YIN

In the solitude after midnight
Can one find a way to outpour anger and obsession?
Those in love now sleep
They lean against each other, circling
One end of the dream to the other.
Those out of love, too, are asleep
Each trying to underscore
Another circular dream of his own.
Between love and its absence
Is a spatial fatigue
Equal in its race with a sky that,
After extending hundreds of rivers and mountains,
Still is unending.

At sunrise
Is there a place for
A tearless face—but crying eyes?
Knowing that you still sleep

Having loved, or not yet having loved,
You know sleep.
We will meet again
After you have loved, or after not loved
Perhaps after wakened and showered
Expecting another lover.
We meet and love, and
Fall into another spatial exhaustion
Like the breaking of an embroidered zither
With fifty, or minus half, of the broken strings
Still an empty chamber of bewilderment
In its solitude.

How, in high noon, or upon what
Would a long, helpless sigh rely?
After bird cries, after tears like blood,
Forever there are strange embraces
Strange departures, and reunions.
After meeting and loving
Forever are the familiar meals
The intimacies, the same old dreams.
Like the morning cry of a desperate cuckoo,
Love still fell on someone else, last evening.

Double Jade Pendant Grievance

(A double pendant is a pair of linked jade rings cut from a piece of hard jade stone. It symbolizes eternal love in a circular form without a beginning or an end.)

Nothing but innocent, stubborn stone, originally,
But ingenious designing
Devout cutting and a craftsman's handling turned
A hard jade stone
Into an inseparable pair
Tiny, delicate rings.
One ring rounds into the other
In the theme of the eternal circle
A complete past enters a complete future
Around the central void
The double event of life
Commingled and confused.
Sorrow and joy
Each with its own beginning and end
The linked two rings are
Sorrow and joy; a perfect metaphor.
Jade is solid, constant

Rings are without end
The perfect gentleman is as pure as jade
And his conviction is as unbroken as a ring.
But the pendant's double design
Mimics irony and fate.
The rings touch each other
Only through a segment of jade,
Like time contacting history
And life is but that passage,
Once events occur, they are history.
One complete past linked to a complete future,
And the central void
Fills with innumerable, relentless regrets,
Unaccountable, broken sorrows.
There was a night
The double jade pendent confirmed love,
There was a song
Exquisite and peerless, a line of which reads:
No one knows, except two hearts.
Another line:
A sharp sword severs the twin-branch in spring.
But the most desperate grievance
Is the pair of couplets in tearless lament:

"A muddy river has its clear days,
And black hair has its time to turn gray;
But as to secret departures and silent farewells,
Each lover is resolved to his fate, having no future
        plans to meet."
In life's mutations
In the innumerable, unaccountable
Secret departures and silent farewells
In the jingling of jade rings hitting each other
And the murmurs of endless cravings and loneliness
There is the suggestion of mutual regret and sympa-
        thy
Beyond history, beyond time
But the double jade pendent grievance
Is a fatal remorse
For history, for the present
Of people and things.

Autumn Meditation

I

A word from a faraway friend arrives, says
There is a separation, in autumn, quite Korean—
"In case you go away, please walk
 On the path of fallen leaves which I have gathered
      for you."
Hundreds of fallen leaves
As many as the varieties of mood;
The most heartbreaking is still the volume on the desk,
Collection of Ten Thousand Leaves,
Especially the one by Kakinomoto Hitomaro:
"In the autumn mountains, yellow leaves are thick,
Mountain paths are misty,
Alas, where shall I seek my love?"
Thus we can see
Ten thousand leaves of words
Are actually ten thousand moods,
Drifting, unattached,
In a foreign land,
In autumn.

A message, following the autumn wind,
Sent from faraway,
Sadly reminding:
I finally dreamt
Under a big tree
The traveling you is autumn,
Leaves profusely falling
Covering your feet
The solitary you is autumn
The silent you is autumn
The sound of autumn is the falling leaves
The hair of autumn is the white reeds
The love of autumn is the lonely pine deep in the
        mountain.

2

Autumn is the dreamy season
Only in the reunion after parting
Can one taste the dream and reality of life
In the joy of staring at one another in silence.
Autumn is the reminiscing season
Only after spring fades and summer withers

And maples turn red, and reed white,
Can one be astonished by a stranger's face in a mirror
And shaken by a flashing glimmer of white hair.
At last the age for reading Tu Fu has come
After the tribulations of wars
The unsettlement of feelings
One is reminded of a lone lantern in the northern
        hill
In an autumnal, solitary night,
"I dare not hope for your chaste celibacy
 But I wish there is always me in you."
Since moving eastward,
There were too many timid thoughts:
Not daring to look back
Dreading deepening anger
Not daring to look ahead
Dreading regretful thoughts.
There is only one daring thought:
On a night when the moon is bright and stars sparse
Putting on a coat
Walking into the backyard to sharpen a sword
I gently recite the first half of a *waka:*
"Loneliness does not

Originate in any one
Particular thing…"

Chrysanthemums

> Clustered chrysanthemums have opened twice,
> in tears of other days.
>> —TU FU
>> (712–770 AD)

Only watching quietly
The unfurling, setting sun
Speedily disappear every evening
Beside the eastern hedge
Would explain the quiet arrival
Of an unknown tear.
Sadness arises on revisiting old places
Regret surges at the mention of past affairs,
They say, only out of an adventurous past
Comes the quiet, unambitious now.
They say, the glistening tears of chrysanthemums
Fall not only for the past
But also for certain illusions.
In the fiction and reality of flower seasons
To search for a good friend
Transcending language and age

Remains a heroic quest, and an illusion.
In life's rainy season
There must have been a stormy downpour,
In life's transient journeys
There must have been a regret
From the clustered chrysanthemums.
Yet after wine, people still argue
How maple woods are injured by the evening dews
And whether the falling tears
Are the chrysanthemums'
Or Tu Fu's.

Mountain Dwelling

Quietly I rinse rice to cook
Then slash a cabbage in halves.
Days of mountain dwelling
Are quite determined and isolated
With coarse tea and plain rice,
Silent days
Words sound clumsy,
Living alone
No need for decorum.
In the cold mountain canyon
Early morning I open the window
There is snow faraway, good.
Late evening, nightfall covers sunset
I do not care.
But there is a regret—
When rain continues for nights
My heart longs for a bunch of fresh cut spring leeks
And the unexpected visit of an old friend
Whom I have not heard from a long time.

Since having long been away from gain and loss,
Fame and disgrace
My mountain dwelling has turned me ordinary
I care not Oe
Nor the Empress Dowager.
Perhaps on the unattached mind
There remains one attachment—
Far in the ocean isles
Are maples still drunk?
Sake still warm?
Heroism still aglow?
And the beautiful faces…
Still charming?

On Reading Keats' "Ode on a Grecian Urn"

Though the same season and weather prevail
The country never ceases changing
There are themes of passion, and of indifference;
Though the same person and personality remain
Stars and events keep mutating
There are plots of joy, and of sadness.
Since departure and reunion remain unpredictable
Loneliness is conspicuous.
This is why one's experience will make an experi-
    enced innocence
No matter how nebulous future endings are
The past remains the cause of all paradox.
The past of the past,
The past of the present,
The past of the future.
Thou still unravished bride of quietness,
Thou foster-child of Silence and slow Time,
The past is a flowery tale
Sweeter than any poetic stanza,

The past is an elegant maid
Graceful as jade.
The pursuit of gods and humans, struggles and escapes
The past—
Wild as ecstasy!
That's why I remain unconvinced by present fears
Or unable to taste melodies unheard
Or love unfelt.
Oh, spirit ditties of no tune!
How can you convey the holding of hands
And the scorching of glances?
How can you retell, in the winter of the northern
        country
A mouthful of snow
Gathered from the fragrant pine
Slowing melting, cool and penetrating?
Lovers who cannot kiss on the Grecian urn!
Of fair girls the loveliest
Hides and will not show herself,
How do you retrace a night
When your hands are upon his shoulders
And your face leans over his chest
Listening to his heartbeat?

The truth of the future is not beauty, but cruelty.
Because the past is the present
Separation is history
Sorrow is despair
Loneliness is bewilderment,
Truth is not beauty, but reality.
And reality is floral snowflakes
Clinging by the window pane on a wintry night
Peeping at the lonely, flickering fire of a lamp.
When the sun rises
Despair becomes truth
Farewell, too, is the truth.

Reading Tao Te Ching, Chapter 20

Since that year I have listened to the Great Way
Knowing that with all training
In liberal and martial arts,
There is no sorting of vice and virtue
Nor right and wrong.
As to the decline of the royal family
And the feudal domination of lords
The social norm spins unbalanced,
Human hearts deceiving
How extremely ridiculous this is
I have pursued the gentleman's way
Among training: archery, horsemanship,
And other rivalries,
Have tried not to be overly competitive
And remaining competitive.
I have eaten coarse food, drunk plain water
Taken wealth as a floating cloud
In the crowded city of *Loyang*
And never feel shame for my rustic dwelling.

As for ascending the spring terrace
Or bathing in the river
Or dreaming of a fond heart dancing in the wind
All have become so remote and indifferent.
If this is so
If I can condition my breath and embrace softness
Can I remain innocent as a new-born babe?
But in every long, bitter night
After reciting the classics and practicing the sword
In me grows, resurgent and impalpable
Like a tide rushing sand, again, on sand
Wave, again, on wave
Voice, again, on voice—
"I am drifting, not knowing where!"
Is it true that for my conscience and integrity
I become dark and dim, in spite of action and
        inaction?
Is it true, oh! Is it really true
The flow of *Tao*
Lies in the bending
Not in the completion of a curve.

Window

If that man quietly passes by your window
Like a night invading
From one row of houses to another
Leaving not a trace,
Nothing happens
Like wintry snow stop falling.

With you inside the window
Is the candle still bright?
Books still heavy in bundles?
Are you still tired, apathetic, and contemplative?
After you have closed your diary
And heaved a sigh
Will you begin to expect and wait?

If nothing did ever happen
Whether this man was known across the four seas
Or left anonymous in this world
If there were no discovery or acquaintance

In the contemplation and expectation of a long night
Would you still rail at his misfortune
And be vexed over his loneliness?
Would you still hear that's man's call to arms and
       frustrations
Far away, by and outside and window?

A Willow Leaf Double Saber

In the winter of 1983, I inadvertently purchased a pair of ancient double sabers at the Great Western gun show in Pomona. In great joy, I hung on to them without releasing my hands. I have been in a foreign country for many years. The meeting between the sabers and me is somewhat like the reunion of two old friends, holding each other's hands, sighing, and inquiring of the past. Though I am a regular patron of gun shows, obtaining these swords was pure coincidence. In a cold night of wintry rain, under a lonely lantern, I examined the sabers and thus wrote this poem.

Tonight how should we retrace our past?
I may have a thousand words of inquiry
But you may not have a single reply
Under the solitary lantern
You silently strip naked
Using the tempered waves of the blades
And irretrievable chips of the edge
Gently to demonstrate a passage of silent China.
An anecdote that history has left out
State affairs

Petty fights
All are contained in our wordless silence.
Yet, when does our reunion start?
Is it this life?
Or was it the last?
I hold you horizontally before me and examine.
Coldly the two willow leaf blades
Are like those knitted brows in the Imperial City
The handles are slender and motley colored
Like the impressions of teeth in the vow of love
Just before the fall of the city.
"Since you have left
My thoughts of you are like the sun and the moon
The sun and the moon flow like water
There is no end."
Gone are the years, changed are the seasons
Even if we meet again, we won't recognize each
     other
Or recount a passion of love
Those moments of life and deaths
How we depended on each other, helping and saving
     each other
How we drifted about in this blood shedding world

To become the one life of the warrior and his
        sabers.
Yet the most heartbreaking of all—
Is the reunion after separation
When we can only sigh, no inquiry
No more pledging of each other's life.
All I have is this remaining life
To repay you for all the forsaken years.

Blue Seas and Mulberry Fields*

In an evening of bitter tea
Let each tell the other of the vicissitudes past
We are the stubborn and the non-regretful ones
Who see drifting as final dwellings,
We are the magnolias bearing creamy flowers
With a pure, simple, petal language
To bloom unrestrained
For an unfaithful summer.
But on those chilly nights, we are
The weak and fragile ones who would cry out—
"Cold!"
Only, no one hears.
We are the lonely and sorrowful one who would
        whisper—
"Chilly!"
Over time, we've learnt hiding our chills in short
        silence
And in transparent tears—

"It was as if I stood under an old deserted temple eaves
Waiting for the rain to stop and resume my journey
But knowing not where the road was."
We are the clan of falling petals
Not knowing where to turn.
There was one summer we fiery bloomed
A host of white flames bursting
People rushed to tell each other.
But in the loneliness of the night
We feel so chilly!
We are the China orphans
Drifting in a foreign land
Seeded from a history, long and in sad plight.
We need a country, intact from divorce
We wander in our parents' separation
And betrothed to the homeless, a gift of history.
Eventually blue sea changes into mulberry fields
And mulberry fields are folded back into blue sea
Only our clamoring monologues
Shiver in the spectrum of history.
Gradually we learnt how to hide honor and disgrace
Love and hatred

Behind the indifference of our eyes:
"Like a wandering mendicant
Traveling far, far away
Never returning…"

*Blue seas and mulberry fields is an allegorical expression in Chinese indicating the transience of time and vicissitude of human affairs.

Wu-hui Monogatari*

If I were to tell first
How many warm tears and deep sighs would I need
To relate a wrong life
With many bold, yet sad incidents?
If, next, you were to supplement
Would you lower your head and start
As in the opening line of *Konjaku Monogatari:*
"At a time not long past..."
Retelling past with *sushi* bars and water fountains
And with an indifferent look
Concluding—"So the tale's been told
And so it's been handed down."
It seems that everyone's past
Is but broken events not worth mentioning
Such as some midnight yearnings
Casual associations of things and events
When it comes to a rosy afternoon
We utter and stutter.
You softly pointed out—

"Deep autumn azaleas are unexpected joy."
But the fragile camellias hint towards a sad ending
Then with what language and gesture
Should we perceive the second coming of flowers?
How, with the holding of hands
Reflection of tears, or touching of lips
Shall we affirm the second arrival of *wu-hui*?
There is a *monogatari* named *Heike*★★
Which opens with the bells at *Gion* temple
And tolls the message of life's evanescence
There is another tale called no remorse
Somewhat like the second blooming of azaleas
Burning in our silent past.

★ *Wu-hui* means "no remorse" in Chinese.
★★ In the *Heike Monogatari*, the Japanese tale begins with,
"The bell of the *Gion* Temple tolls into every man's heart
to warn him that all is vanity and evanescence. The faded
flowers of the *sala* trees by the Buddha's death-bed bear
witness to the truth that all who flourish are destined to
decay. Yes, pride must have its fall, for it is as insubstantial
as a dream on a spring night. The brave and violent man—
he too must die away in the end, like a whirl of dust in
the wind."

Midnight Is My Song

Between midnight and dawn,
Between waking and drifting back to dreams,
Is the feeling ignorant how to be disposed,
And the regret not knowing how to smooth out;
Especially, a life there—
Cannot reminisce all, or retell.
Endless drifting, wanderings among time,
As it thickens with the midnight dews,
Cold and chilly, quite to the bone.
Between moon set and sun-rising dawn,
Aspiration and worry for one's country
Arousing and exciting:
Self, the self, to be identified!
Nation, the nation, to be recognized!
Life, a life, to be realized!
Country, a country, to become strong!
A foreign midnight
Is an unoccupied, frustrating nostalgic hour.
When one is middle-aged, at life's midnight,

There is an unspeakable silence.
When there is, somewhat, a call
Seeming to come from the void,
To which you do not know how to respond
For you do not know how to listen;
Somewhat a song, at midnight
Abruptly bursts into flames like a wildfire
That defies the time to narrate
And mocks the telling voice:
"Let midnight be the prelude of dawn,
Let me wake from dreams' ocean
To wade to reality's beach;
Let me push wide the door of history
And throw myself into the azure gleams of the
        Chinese;
Let me know cold dews, dark nights only tempo-
        rarily;
Evil words gusting like winds will not bend
The green silent growth of grass.
If I weep,
Let me know for what;
If I rejoice,
Let me know for whom;

If I lack words,
Tell me none are needed.
Let me be patient
Let me wait
Constant as a bronze statue,
Endless as a fountain;
Let my loyal innocence
Impede flowing time
And bestow upon me those belated,
But ascertained, inevitable blessings."

Reincarnation

"Would that be an extravagant wish,
After a few reincarnations,
To want to lie by your pillow side,
And listen to your private talk
At midnight, with no one around?"
If this reunion is cause for nothing,
Then what consequence could follow our departure?
Is it really true that every cause is
Consequence in cycle, and again?
If our unions are reunions,
All are natural, beyond pretense,
Just as in what night when, tears in your eyes,
You nestled a face in your hands, attentively scruti-
        nizing
With so much love and regret,
And afterward said,
"I have waited long for you."
Why is such a face so familiar
And its contours so refined?

The outpouring love of your eyes
Harmonizes, reconciles every kind of night.
Something must have happened
Seven days ago, seven years,
Or seven lifetimes;
Something was said,
Some wish made,
Or some promises.
Oh! Some love must have been unrequited—
Perhaps sleeping apart from the same pillow or
        blanket,
Or sharing no days of hardship
When there was need to stand and protect
You in feebleness, or helplessness.
Yet, you received some joys,
In fleeting moments, in the flashes of lightning,
Or in dreams of hallucinations:
Some days flowered
Like a cluster of red daisies,
Quietly bloomed to the wind.
After the floral season, the buds are still many,
Host after host,
Continuation after continuation;

For only such cycles can make one fluctuate
In the angry sea of life and death,
To receive unjustly all the stormy blows of
        karma—
Until one night
You turned and looked at a face,
Tears bursting like hot volcano lava, and said,
"For heaven's sake,
We've waited such a long time,
And finally meet again."

The Panther

Those tiresome eyes,
And supple, wide strides
Facing the iron bars of reality
Behind is the blank universe
Of course, everything is attributed to Rilke!
But the thirst and hunger in those eyes,
Because stars have come and gone,
Moons have risen and fallen;
Because of hundreds of thousands of watching eyes,
There is now the riveting now on these two,
And each stares indulgently:
From the side glance of the ringlets, following the ear,
To the focus on a drop of sweat
On the tip of the nose.
Fatigue! Oh! Are those anticipating years
Unapproachable,
Unable to be intimate.
Oh! Softly are the recollection of wide strides,
The lonely years of majestic wandering,

Endless forests,
Tedious nights;
Beyond stars are still stars,
Beyond moons are still moons,
Tree shadows like a hundred bars,
One leap, and all become winds at the back.
No doubt, this is *Jardin des Plantes en Paris,*
Also the glass menagerie,
Also the world circus.
Although the claws are still sharp,
And muscles flex as a bent bow.

Tiburon, California

After a prolonged illness,
Sailing to Tiburon sounds adventurous.
A past friend, with his past house
Is now a mirage of glamour.
This may shock, may dizzy some,
But the visit is casual
With a secret desire to meet;
One heart is indebted from kindness,
And another full of sacrificial rituals,
As the setting sun is facing the lonely mountain
Or like the spring water running around the pier,
Such is the feeling
Void of words to tell
Void of reasons to unravel,
Such is the case,
Although there was intimacy between lovers
And warm tears within a long, cold night,
Such is the case,
The morning coffee was drunk

With little attention to the morning news,
Because this is Tiburon,
Peninsula of the past,
At the tip-end of human feelings;
Further on is the endless ocean,
Which is why we can only look back in Tiburon,
Never forward, never using a present to analyze the
    past,
Because what was then strange
Now is intimate;
What was a separation of months and years
Now is togetherness in seconds and minutes,
Such is the case
Were there a pledge between the coast and the tides,
It would mean only a lifetime of suffering.
But in every night of a full moon,
Tides still rush from the Orient to San Francisco,
Golden Gate in front,
Angel Island at left,
Tiburon on the right;
There are people who still persist
About legendary death and resurrection, because
"This is a land full of hope,

Also a land full of despair,
A city full of joy,
Also a city of sorrow everywhere…"

Dream Cutting Sword

Among the rivers and lakes, people used to say:
It is easier to cut heads than to cut feelings,
If cutting feelings is difficult,
Cutting dreams is ever more so.

Since the unhappy days with wine,
I practice swords, study books, and make friends.
A recluse from the life of vengeance and *seppuku*,
I drink wine in autumn,
Eat crabs, and grow chrysanthemums,
And now know
Dreams do not happen merely at night;
Even the waking from dreams,
It does not need to take place in the garden.
Since you left,
My lute strings are broken,
No more news about you,
While reading underneath the house eaves;
There is always a jealousy before closing a book,

A regret for giving up one's beloved stallion,
By the faraway misty waves.

If a sword can cut dreams,
It's because the remaining dream is nowhere to be
        found,
What the sword cannot sever
Is the source of thought—
Appearing and disappearing
Thought comes, a dream appears,
Thought goes, a dream disappears,
Without a trace.

Pink Cheeks

When did you become an oriole of the day
And start reminiscing the nocturnes?
When did you become afraid of sad tunes
And drop your head to weep silently?
May be, the fluctuating events of life
Were all in the beginning inevitable truths,
But afterwards, were merely illusory recollections.
May be, the nights of passion in early days
Have become the bitter poems in this later stage.
This is why many silent nights have
Luring, lonely pulsation,
A voice vaguely calling then, it seems—
"If I sing,
Will you listen?"
Another yearning—
"What then is an eternal song?"
In fact,
Songs of the orioles,
Sad tunes,

Passionate nights,
Bitter poems,
All are silent confessions of a drifting wanderer.
Silent, because the world will not understand,
As Tu Fu's poem on pink cheeks,
Or Basho's *haiku* on late spring and departure:
"Who will understand
The tears of fish crying in water,
Or the sad songs of birds in the woods?"
It sounds as though in numerous lonely evenings
There must be more torture, more in separation,
Before there can be revealed deep love.
It seems as though deep chiseling love and hate
Are as conspicuous as hot summers and cold autumns.
Like you once replied,
        "What is the use of only fondness?"
Then down the rain began to sprinkle,
Outside the window to fall,
On the stairs,
On the remote heart of a drifter.
You turned inside the closed the door,
Putting all your farewells and longings
Into the tunes you once forgot.

Redondo Beach in Evening Rain

People who came to watch high tides are now
      dispersed,
The drapes of night are fallen,
But the dramatic plots of the coastline
Are still long and misty.
Listen! They say this is the tune of the poet
In Dover Beach, and his affirmations—
The onflow of tides
Are tragedies of the Aegean Sea,
Telling of heroic uncertainty,
And the great resurrection of love.

But what appears to be the saddest is still—
After climbing the steps, and
Turning with a farewell look,
What is gone I can only recollect,
But not looking back
Is like embracing torrents of the past
You cannot detain,

Can only flow along, like the intoxication of wine,
Dizzy and confused.

Two lives, touching upon each other,
Become the silent, whirling eddies,
Two pairs of eyes, bidding helpless farewells,
Become the clamoring ocean tides,
Mid-aged tales of danger,
Wave after wave,
United in a common theme
But in different performances
With a hundred kinds of dialogues,
Voicing one bound mood,
The incoming tides chant a chorus,
The outgoing tides
Stutter interior monologues.

Promises

Those promises, made in the early years
Still grow green and freshen like
Spring plains, stretching from
The verdant, colorful brush of sprinkling rain
To the thick woods of autumn,
"So many promises,
Nothing but empty promises!"
Even the dignified, falling golden leaves
And the quietude of woods
Render slight commentaries.

Those trips, promised in the early years,
Still flex with heroic feelings,
The Scottish highlands, wavering with
Bagpipes beats and swirling plaid,
Jump high and low;
The unsettled weather of the mind
Grows bright, grows dark,
Crisscrossing squares

Like the plaid-colored kilts.
As to the azure Mediterranean
And the heavy, sweetened Brazil,
"So many promises,
Nothing but empty promises!"
Except for the starlight of Paris
After an evening recitation under a chilled moon
While, in the mirror trembling in the hand
Fine temple hairs glisten beside the sideburns.

The only promise that can be promised repeatedly
        today
Is a vast piece of lovely land
From the rain-drizzling Keelung
Winding and sprinkling
Along the seacoast
Stretching into the lean, graceful tip of the Goose
        Nose,
So many summer fruits clustered there!
They are not empty!
Nor are the wintry vegetables, in abundance!
As to those journeys and promises in early years,
They are merely lush poetic nihilism of youthful days.

Cliff House

Cannot say at what time
The owner finally decided
To build a square house
By the edge of the steep cliff by the ocean;
Maybe four strong walls are unsurpassed
Against all coming storms into the bay,
So they may extend
An invitation to all San Francisco visitors
To become a temporary witness.

Perhaps since the decision to build,
Every rushing tide and undercurrent
Intimately confers with the cliff house;
Every inch of quiet erosion
Whispering to the house's foundation.
Only those distressed lovers
Shuttling back and forth in time,
Infatuated with the full frontal scenic view
Come gathering from all places

At a suggested proposal to elope,
Perhaps, at a rumored, crumbling love.
At least, out on the capricious ocean breezes
Historical secrets incessantly echo.

In one cold spring season
A young woman sadly retells—
She drank coffee and liquor in the cliff house,
There were bright days, wet days,
At dawn, and at dusk…
Past days float, then sink in the memory sea,
To pound and rush with the intricacy of love and hate,
Unperceivable as the sea's depth,
Sometimes cold and gray and full of hatred and sorrow,
Sometimes clear and blue like a sound dream…

Another anecdote:
On a chilly afternoon
A homeless drifter
Quietly uses the remaining bitter coffee in his mug
To resist a love story on Chopin.
He has bet ten stormy years
Against a night of quiet farewell.

All those who move about the cliff house
Will be reminded of unions and past departures,
Happiness and sorrows in the future…

That is why all the time
The visitors of the cliff house inquire,
Since coming is a dream, and going a void,
Life and affairs—
Only a segment of the unending past events,
Why do we still have to look into—
Where are you coming from?
Where am I going?
Numerous encounters and meetings
Are only necessities of fate!
They are like the violent tides beating on the cliff,
Slashing hundreds of inerasable wounds on life.
Once the stars are spread out in the wide plain,
And the moon rushes out in the great lake,
The cliff house will stand imposingly high,
Leaving all events in its walls
To the unpredictable sea wind,
Bringing them softly to the misty, faraway future.

One After My Own Heart

Passing from the old people's narratives,
Generation through generation,
Such an old legendary tale
Happened in ancient time,
In the early Chinese Republic,
And most frequent in modern times.
Intricate feelings of a lifetime,
After an evening of lute,
Become an incessant flow of stream
Coming from nowhere,
Going nowhere.
Water runs like a midnight narration,
Fluent, but choked with emotions:
It's indeed difficult to find an understanding friend!
You owe me a segment of the sword dance,
I owe you a movement from the lute tune,
Oh, lute and sword are never meant to join!
Because—
Music is intrinsically hard to understand,

But more difficult
Is to find in a person real understanding.
The lute clings
Like falling leaves and petals—
There is an inch of a heart
With no one to share,
"Wishing the wind to disperse the clouds
And telling the moon by the end of the sky,
I bring my lute to ascend the pavilion,
The pavilion is high, and the moon is full,
While the love-longing tune is unfinished,
My tears drop, and strings break."
Bright, colorful tunes,
Shadows of fantastic dreams,
Even a brief moment of reunion
Is the prearrangement of providence.
Because—
One can be considered a good musician
Only after performing a thousand tunes;
A collector of arms becomes a connoisseur
Only by viewing a thousand swords.
When we met again,
It was also the end of spring,

The snow began to melt.
Whatever landscape emerged from the sword,
Whatever feelings hummed and swirled from the lute,
These are mere broken legends for later days.
As to those who really went to seek the truth,
They may search only from the heavy and light
        plucking of strings,
Or from the sharp double-edged blades of love and
        hate.

Outflow

Always there is the outflow of tears
Between brimming and dropping.
For a past life,
The details of which are not worth telling,
But the past complexity
Entwined in its branches
Reaching, linking to the present.
From Heng-yang Road
And turning into Chungking South Road,
There are cool sweet watermelon juices,
And iced-cold sour plum drinks.

From *Forbidden Games*
Turning into Ravel's *Bolero*,
Always there is the outflow of joy.
A reunion after disaster is worth celebrating,
Is precious in the wordless moments of facing one
    another.
Those separated are united,

Those drifted now returned,
A solitary boat, sailing half-life in raging waves
Finally glides one night into a haven.
The sound of waves in the dark ocean
Has never been so tender and tempting.
Confused starlight vie to testify to the sky—
A snow-white beach
Following the beats of tides,
Strips itself nude to a belated crescent moon.

A Name Seal

An unexpected guest came that year,
Amidst the hurried farewells,
A name seal had been left, along with years of youth,
Receding in the misty ripples of a study desk.
In a glimpse, there go a few years—
Pigeons in the square,
Sunlight and cactus flowers,
All but a dreamy mirage by the bay.
In weeping, telling drizzles
And lamenting sea breezes,
In memory they call incessantly in the mirage of life.
A few years' time
Indeed change, indeed can be clouds, then rain,
Just as a guest suddenly awakens
And formerly fate's envoy, becomes a master of life.
While he who was the host
Deliberately now, in his middle-aged years, forsakes his
    name,
Tries even through his unredeemable error as he is

To see the bitter love he had as he was.
His future, where he may live,
Floating like a duckweed,
And so goes life.
By logic, because the guest is now host,
The host should be guest.
Reminiscing old affairs,
Thoughts grow uncontrolled.
As to how to return the past to the future,
For a passing guest who simply wants to forget his
        name
It is a tough problem.
Seasons past,
Dreams like dust,
The solution is to return the past to the past,
The future will then accommodate the present.

The Watch

This is an automatic, electronic watch,
Forever pointing to the present,
Never recalling the past,
Nor worrying the future,
Always, twelve to twelve,
Merely a circle
Beginning from the unknown,
Fading into another unknown.
Slow and unyielding
Events comprise each minute and second,
And fade away for others,
Each minute and second
Is a slashing wound in life,
Bright red scars branding into long memories,
When they accrete as a lifetime,
And everything suddenly is history.
Like a cluster of grapes of wrath,
Sweet and sour, each grape
Is a backward glance at the past,

One after another taken from the whole,
Small clusters are chapters,
Beginning with childhood,
Then a barren trellis, plucked, old age;
Starting with love,
Then an absence from the whole.
Circles, circles of complete history,
Twelve to twelve,
In the beginning, the clamor of bright sunlight,
The heroic challenge of the present for a future,
Rash, hurried,
Forceful and persistent,
Each minute and second,
Like dew and like lightning,
Like dream and like illusion,
Until the past quietly emerges
With a mother's tender patience
To attend to the final act,
To wipe tears, give ointment for the wound,
And silently record happy events.
Then the moon brightens stars to scarceness,
Black crows begin their southward flight,
The deeper the wound, the further midnight dreams go.

"Oh, with the turning and turning in the
        deepening gyre,
The hovering falcon
Can hear no more the call of the falconer!"
Now is already past,
The future is beyond the falconer's sight,
The falcon hovers farther, farther,
The turning gyre, dreamland, chills.
Only the long arm of the automatic electronic
        watch
Firmly defines a position,
Murmuring each second, each word—
"Life is but a passage of time,
Life is but a passage of song,
Be quiet no longer."

Heidegger! Heidegger!

Like submerging into a thousand-fathom ocean,
Beginning is in slow descent,
Sunlight glaring into the eyes,
And a warm flow of current,
Then it is blue, and dark green,
Weeping and yelling as in a dense downpour of rain,
Pounding eardrums,
Compression and throbbing beats,
And the heart finally stops—
Like submerging into a thousand-fathom ocean,
Beginning is the undulating, entangling seaweed,
In green and russet red;
Fishes weaving to and fro,
Back and forth like confused recollections.
Colorful fishes!
Colorful memory of life!
Slowly fading, becoming silent,
Slowly descending in silence,
This is the arrival of the cold, dark night

Ceasing life,
Ceasing time;
Cold sea bottom,
Chilly dark night.
What is to emerge in space
Is an unyielding dreamland,
Starting from the ancient border Loulan,
Moving toward the faraway Chang-an,
Turning into the prosperous Loyang.
The three thousand threads of golden locks on the pil
Once caused distress;
They were once as soft, as long as the silk route,
But now the camel bells are silent,
The horse hooves no longer gallop,
And the magnificent procession of T'ang travelers,
Before being buried by the sand storm of the desert,
Had already been silenced by the stopping of time.
Oh! Life is only a passage of time!
And time exists only in being alive!
The flow of life is to merge with a greater life,
The consciousness of Being,
Is to be connected to a greater Being.
Individual existence

Is a self Being;
Individual life
Is a self apparition;
Loulan, Chang-an, and Loyang
Fair maiden, flesh, hair, and soil,
When life's being ceases
Time stops.
One thousand years, or six thousand years,
It makes no difference.
Like submerging into a thousand-fathom ocean,
Floating, descending, silently,
Time echoes time,
Wavering into ripples of infinite space,
Expanding, fluctuating, resting,
Until a thousand generations later,
An expedition of archaeologists starts with piles
        of ancient scrolls,
Pushing present back into the past,
Oblivion back into recollection,
Like a seed buried deep beneath the snow,
Under the caressing, digging fingers,
A dream begins slowly to unfurl,
To bloom into colorful flowers of history,

Then the camel bells chime again,
Hooves of horses gallop again,
Noises in the silk route,
Oh! Heidegger, Heidegger!

A Fish Fossil

After you have decided to retrace to me
The intertwining complexity of half your life's past,
What is revealed
Is our forever bewildered infinite future.
What has been spacious blue seas
Now is acre upon acre of mulberry fields,
But without those eyes,
How can we have those sorrowful tears?
Without the flesh,
How can we have the painful teeth marks of love?
Thus, in innumerable chilly midnights,
We can only silently sit and sob,
Face each other wordlessly,
As if telling everything is useless,
And not telling is useless.
There seems always to be an unfinished story
In one's life,
Starting with pitying and admiring,
Ending with loving and separating.

As if in the sad recollection of events,
Despite how tragic and sorrowful when they occurred
Afterwards, there is really nothing to tell.
Even there is something to tell,
But mere witty deceits of the world,
And unyielding love.
As if in such a brevity of life,
Nothing is that important,
Particularly one's life with another's;
Over an ever-changing billion or trillion years
They are fallen leaves slowly sinking into the riverbed,
Softly, submissively, and wordlessly,
Without help, without choice,
Because what can be chosen or confused
Can happen only in one lifetime.
Beyond one life,
All sorrowful and sentimental affairs of the past
Will engrave in the memory of changing time,
Like a fish fossil!
Fish fossil,
In the solidification of time,
Will you still recall
All the sound and fury of the past,

And the dreams and regrets of events?
Was it true that when the stream dried up
And you were stranded on land,
You tried to spew and wet each other?
Was it true that the only thing you could not do
Was to forget each other in the rivers and lakes?
In those years
A little caring
Was a cool, soothing drizzle;
A light embrace,
Would always bring waves of touched emotions.
In those years,
We vowed to each other—
Until the rocks rot, and the seas go dry,
Our love will never regret!
But we could never explain
Why tears in our eyes,
Or despair in our dropping heads.
It seemed that if the stream's drying up was fate,
Being stranded on land also was,
It seemed as though we were forever the weaker race,
Forever gentle, forever being taken advantage of.
It seemed that in the free universe

We were the ones more easily caught and hurt.
We had been born in an age when life was not as good
    as death,
And lived in a century when to live was better than to
    die.
We argued,
We forgave,
But we seemed to understand clearly—
Only those who went through thick and thin
Would treasure tiny caresses and embraces.
This is why in numerous chilly midnights
We kept silent, sobbed, and faced each other word-
    lessly,
And unwilling to separate!
Now we finally understand,
The unending sorrow of separation
Can be witnessed only by a fish fossil,
Only beyond the old speculation and hypotheses
Of archaeologists and biologists
Can we retrace a broken mythical legend—
This was a wandering fish,
Drifting away from the China seas,
Everywhere his country is loneliness,

His home is in the tides,
He uses the rapid countercurrents of his fate
To splash up the floral waves of his youth;
What is hiding deep in his heart
As the eagerness for a final dwelling
And the regrets of not returning,
Will eventually follow the mutation of time
Petrifying into an indifferent, wordless fossil.

Beauty of Imperfection

They say imperfection results from pursuing perfection.
It was like that early morning sunlight
Sparsely shining through the dense bamboo and
    timber woods,
Sprinkling, wholeheartedly pouring on a cliff
Thickly clothed in verdant moss,
Somewhat, there remain last night's dews, vaguely
Clinging to your remaining, repeated concern,
As up and down you tread in childhood memory;
Suddenly, blanketed by a rushing mountain fog
You turn, unaware,
To try to speak to someone, presuming that
There is one who understands what you wish to tell—
Those beauties!
But there is no one there,
Because you don't want those whom you can have,
Those whom you can, you don't want to have,
Those imperfections!
Huge trees over the hills,

Bellflowers everywhere
In the cool, mysterious blowing of a mountain breeze,
And intermittent croaking of frogs;
Unaware, you stop
To try to say to someone—"Listen!"
As if all the secrets in the whole wide world
Are to be shared by two persons only.

Therefore, imperfection is part perfection.
Somewhat like an incomplete life is lived,
Somewhat like the night after we have tasted spring tea,
When after a long awakening of night,
There seems to be a voice,
Whirling and inquiring:
Why didn't we belong to China of old?
Why did we drift so far away?
Why are life's twirling eddies so wonderful?
Those who left will return,
Those set apart will be reunited,
Eventually some passages will be written
To serve witness to the beauty of imperfection
As sad and affectionate as poetry,
Realistic and magical as fiction.

Yearning

Like wiping off layers of dense, misty fog,
Chopping away barriers of distressing brambles,
You finally made up your mind, toiling at a task—
To love and to make it work
Like the silent, tenacious growing of the green moss,
To spread, and to grope,
And let its greenness fill a gray, sorrowful heart.

In the emptiness of the dark night,
Bringing along a somewhat illusory blessing,
You began to yearn and call my names,
One after another, again and again,
Like a mother yearning for her child,
Like river tides settled by the town of sunset,
As if calling is possessing,
And all names are simply eager variants in recent years,
Eager for one after your own heart,
Eager for spiritual attachments,
Each calling seeming to say:

Why is it never mine?
Why are all these names, given and self, said thus?
Why have we met so late?
But is our yearning so full of thirst and hunger?
Why would it be a time, when my life is in its full tide
Appearing in such an irresolute you?

In the overlapping of love and departure,
In the drowsiness of dream and waking,
I seem to hear your incessant, echoing cries:
These names are full of crime and punishment,
Karma and shame—
An ungrateful son,
An unfaithful husband,
An unrighteous father,
An encaged, domesticated beast,
Unabashedly exposing his clumsy cowardice,
And stretching out his hand for help.
A huge error,
Falling into another's hands
Definitely becomes the other's huge error.
This is why such a name has neither "forever"
Nor the possessive pronoun "yours,"

Because it represents an absolute courage,
Absolute maturity,
Absolute lost!
Its sounds like existentialism,
Or Lao Tzu and Chuang Tzu,
Or an afternoon tea,
Or a couple of borrowed books.

Maple Leaf Watermarks

Alongside the cobbled path,
Next to a smear of brilliant, verdant moss,
Patches of watermarks,
Shapes like palms of maple leaves—
They seem like what refuses to be forgotten
Never will disappear;
Wounds and scars of one's life,
Despite how they hide beneath the wintry moss,
With an intention or not, always revealing
To this world a message:
Life once as fiery as the maple
Forever scorches and brands one's memory.

But, every time we met, why did we
Know certainly only the following departure?
Why after departure was there only the uncertain
Next meeting?
Why does fate hold everything?
Why the entanglement in

Such obvious, bitter love?
Is it necessary to evade
Offering of obvious protection and happiness?
Did you have to postpone your love for a man?
To await pity, giving it to his white hairs?
To wait until the best poem was composed?
Why does love need two identities,
But one status?
"I bring with me a bosom of joy and hope,
To give you light and warmth,
I secretly pondered,
It was such a conflicting, a difficult matter
For a shy, dignified you to come from faraway,
You must have decided and undecided—
To come, not to come,
Though I treasure every past moment,
And anticipate each from the future,
Yet what you wrestle in shyness right now
Is how to break a promise."
"Why does remorse lengthen itself in your deep sigh?
Why do hesitant, dreamy eyes always mark your face?
Why is it that, were there love,
It never should be between two cities?

When the country crumbles,
Shouldn't we bear the survivors' contrition?
Why did you have to wait all these long years,
As you have waited for the best poet
Before choosing me?"

But in the countless cold evenings at the academy,
Hands pushing open the door make such a dreary
      gesture!
It's already night, but not knowing night,
It's loneliness, but keep fearing loneliness
And becoming sorrowful in loneliness,
Even refusing loneliness!
You raised your head to look around,
Falling leaves fluttering and dancing,
Leaves clamoring on the ground;
But no one here beside you
Circled her left hand around your right arm.
The wind kept blowing,
The rain drizzled,
You lowered your head and walked alone,
With no one's notice,
No one's respect,

No one's recognition.
You are one of the many fallen maple leaves,
In scarlet, blood-stained color.
You are China's pain hidden in her heart,
Drifting in a foreign land,
Leaving all causes to the determinism of autumn.
Perhaps these are the joy and sorrow of a middle-aged
    man,
The bright spring days
Forever wait to belong to youngsters.
Everyone must have budded, blossomed, and foliaged,
Must have once so eagerly stretched branches out to
    the blue.
But now come the stage of the maple leaf watermarks:
"If it were loneliness,
It would forever be loneliness."
There is a slight sigh,
Then, both hands tightly to the lapels,
You disappear in a hurried night, rain, and wind.

The Last Love Poem

Like the fluency of torn silk,
The cleavage, once having begun to tear,
Will irrevocably head towards separation.
I have never been good at counting time,
But in order to measure our partition,
I have begun to count by the years.
Is it really true that you require your final departure
So you may reveal my countless regrets?

"You are someone in my mind,
By the south of the great sea,
Who asked: What shall I send back to you?
Kerchief, hairpins, double-jade ring pendants?
Verdant ceramic bowls?
Beads from a monastery?
I heard that you've loved someone else,
But how could I have so stonehearted
Burnt them all?
Discarded them all?"

I dally with each thing of remembrance—
Stationeries, bookmarks, notebooks,
And a long, long poem.
I have never been good in retracing time,
But I seem to recall
A segment entitled "Opus 1–7".

My ultimate regret
Is not really in our separation,
But in my final loneliness.

In the great seas, north and south,
There is no such wind
That can so swiftly move a sailing urge of reunion.
There is no such language
That can exceed each other's sorrowful silence.
We fought, envious, rejected by the world,
We were partial, stubborn, and unable to take each
    other.
Numerous nights
We shouted, raised our fists,
"From now on, not a thought for each other!"

But in endless days and nights,
Feelings like what was written in that note:
"After fire extinguishes,
Ashes are still warm."
The last love poem
Is like the last leaf falling at autumn's end,
When all the past flowery glory
Is left to the lonely trunk of the tree.
They said: Love deluges in this world.
They said: Poets begin to worry for their country.
They again told each other:
Since Genesis, there has been no poetry to touch the
    heart.

I have never been good at getting even,
But I still am fond of a certain restraint and tenderness,
As is in the poems of Hsi Muren.

GREEN INTEGER
6026 Wilshire Boulevard
Los Angeles, California 90036
(213) 857-1115 FAX: (213) 857-0143
E-Mail: djmess@sunmoon.com
Visit Our New Web-Site: www.sunmoon.com

GREEN INTEGER
Pataphysics and Pedantry

Edited by Per Bregne
Douglas Messerli, *Publisher*

Essays, Manifestos, Statements, Speeches, Maxims,
Epistles, Diaristic Notes, Narratives, Natural Histories,
Poems, Plays, Performances, Ramblings, Revelations
and all such ephemera as may appear necessary
to bring society into a slight tremolo of confusion
and fright at least.

*

Green Integer Books

History, or Messages from History Gertrude Stein [1997]
Notes on the Cinematographer Robert Bresson [1997]
The Critic As Artist Oscar Wilde [1997]
Tent Posts Henri Michaux [1997]
Eureka Edgar Allan Poe [1997]
An Interview Jean Renoir [1998]
Mirrors Marcel Cohen [1998]
The Effort to Fall Christopher Spranger [1998]
Radio Dialogs I Arno Schmidt [1999]
Travels Hans Christian Andersen [1999]
In the Mirror of the Eighth King Christopher Middleton [1999]
On Ibsen James Joyce [1999]
Laughter: An Essay on the Meaning of the Comic Henri Bergson [1999]

Seven Visions Sergei Paradjanov [1998]

Ghost Image Hervé Guibert [1998]

Ballets Without Music, Without Dancers, Without Anything [1999]
Louis-Ferdinand Céline [1999]

My Tired Father Gellu Naum [1999]

Manifestos Manifest Vicente Huidobro [1999]

On Overgrown Paths Knut Hamsun [1999]

What Is Man? Mark Twain [2000]

Metropolis Antonio Porta [1999]

Poems Sappho [1999]

Hell Has No Limits José Donoso [1999]

Theoretical Objects Nick Piombino [1999]

Art *Poetic'* Olivier Cadiot [1999]

Fugitive Suns: Selected Poetry Andrée Chedid [1999]

Mexico. A Play Gertrude Stein [2000]

Sky-Eclipse: Selected Poems Régis Bonvicino [2000]

The Resurrection of Lady Lester OyamO [2000]

Crowtet I: A Murder of Crows and *The Hyacinth Macaw*
Mac Wellman [2000]

Abingdon Square María Irene Fornes [2000]

The Masses Are Asses Pedro Pietri [2000]

*Three Masterpieces of Cuban Drama: Plays by Julio Matas,
Carlos Felipe, and Virgilio Piñera* edited with an Introduction
by Luis F. González-Cruz and Ann Waggoner Aken [2000]

Drifting Dominic Cheung (Chang Ts'o) [2000]

Green Integer EL-E-PHANT Books
[6 × 9 format]

The PIP Anthology of World Poetry of the 20th Century 1 (2000)
edited with a Preface by Douglas Messerli
readiness / enough / depends / on Larry Eigner (2000)

BOOKS FORTHCOMING FROM GREEN INTEGER

Islands and Other Essays Jean Grenier
Operatics Michel Leiris
The Doll and *The Doll at Play* Hans Bellmer
[with poetry by Paul Éluard]
Water from a Bucket Charles Henri Ford
American Notes Charles Dickens
To Do: A Book of Alphabets and Birthdays
Gertrude Stein
Letters from Hanusse Joshua Haigh
[edited by Douglas Messerli]
Prefaces and Essays on Poetry
William Wordsworth
Licorice Chronicles Ted Greenwald
The Complete Warhol Screenplays
Ronald Tavel
Confessions of an English Opium-Eater
Thomas De Quincey
The Renaissance Walter Pater
Venusburg Anthony Powell
Captain Nemo's Library Per Olav Enquist

Selected Poems and Journal Fragments Maurice Gilliam
Utah Toby Olson
The Twofold Vibration Raymond Federman [2000]
The Pretext Rae Armantrout [2000]
Gold Fools Gilbert Sorrentino [2000]
Against Nature J. K. Huysmans
Satyricon Petronius [translation ascribed to Oscar Wilde]
The Cape of Good Hope Emmanuel Hocquard
The Antiphon Djuna Barnes
Traveling through Brittany Gustave Flaubert
Delirum of Interpretations Fiona Templeton